Pageant

ALSO BY JOANNA FUHRMAN:

Moraine
Ugh Ugh Ocean
Freud in Brooklyn

Pageant

JOANNA FUHRMAN

ALICE JAMES BOOKS
Farmington, Maine

10 9 8 7 6 5 4 3 2 1

Alice James Books are published by Alice James Poetry Cooperative, Inc.,
an affiliate of the University of Maine at Farmington.

ALICE JAMES BOOKS
238 MAIN STREET
FARMINGTON, ME 04938

www.alicejamesbooks.org

Library of Congress Cataloging-in-Publication Data:
  Fuhrman, Joanna, 1972-
  Pageant / Joanna Fuhrman.
    p. cm.
  Poems.
  ISBN 978-1-882295-77-7
  I. Title.
  PS3556.U3247P34 2009
  811'.54--dc22
                      2009037580

Alice James Books gratefully acknowledges support from individual donors,
private foundations, the University of Maine at Farmington and the National
Endowment for the Arts. 🌱

Cover art: Ida Applebroog, *Jimmy Choo Progeny*, 2005
Inkjet on moulin de larroque paper, 22 3/8 x 12 3/4 inches
Edition #: BAT

Photo credit: Emily Poole

ACKNOWLEDGMENTS

Many thanks to the editors of the publications where versions of some of these poems originally appeared:

American Letters & Commentary, "You Don't Mean That Gesture, She Said"

Boog City, "Knots," "Stagflation" and "Why Are All the Elephants Crying?"

Big Game Review, "A Woman Wears a Nose Like a Lost Dwelling"

Conduit, "The Shaman Figurine Car Ornament Explains the Accident, Then Naps" and "The Automythologist Takes a Vacation"

Court Green, "Fuzzy Parable with Gin Fizz"

eoagh, "Testimony" and "This Is What I Meant when I Said My Memories Are Not Exactly True"

Exquisite Corpse, "Facts for Survival"

Filter, "How to Be Happy" and "The Magic Puppy Dog Biscuit Predicts the Return of Fall"

Hanging Loose, "On Some Gossip Overheard at the Meritocracy Bar and Grill"; "The Summer We Were All Seventeen"; "Planetary Notebook"; "Rock the Hothouse, Loot the Brain"; "By the Skeletons of Hurdygurdy Monkeys and Other Journeys Toward Nanotechnology"; "Portrait on Expired Film"; "The Car Door Squeaks Because I'm 32"; "The Lecture"; "Boots, Mistletoes, Cookies and Thumbs" and "The 22nd Century"

Jacket, "At the Evil Boss Convention"

La Fovea, "Forgiveness" and "Song with Borrowed Shoes"

New American Writing, "Broken Song with Light Bulb Tail"

Ocho, "Plain Sight," "The Joke," "For Newlyweds" and "Unnamed Street with Five Fingers and a Box"

Pig, "And Yes, I Would Like Another Ghost-shaped Truffle!" and "Uniforms Are Sexy Too"

Scapegoat Review, "The Joke," "The Writer's Life" and "Poem in Favor of Joy"

Traffic, "There's No Kindness," "I Don't Live Here Often, She Said" and "For Janet Richmond, Who I Think Hated Elegies"

Vanitas, "The New Realism" and "Ode to Television"

"Fuzzy Parable with Gin Fizz" was republished in the Spout Press anthology *Lush: A Poetry Anthology and Cocktail Guide.*

"The Shaman Figurine Car Ornament Explains the Accident, Then Naps"; "The Magic Puppy Dog Biscuit Predicts the Return of Fall"; "You Don't Mean That Gesture, She Said"; "Uniforms Are Sexy Too" and "Why Are All the Elephants Crying?" were republished in a chapbook titled *Clone School* published by Big Game Books. Thanks to Maureen Thorson for the beautiful work.

Thanks to Bob Kerr for his endless support and inspiration.

I would especially like to thank Donna Brook, Idra Novey and Jean-Paul Pecqueur for their help with the manuscript. Thanks and love to the editors of Hanging Loose Press for their many years of support and encouragement.

TABLE OF CONTENTS

The New Realism   1

Ode to Television   2

The Summer We Were All Seventeen   4

Plain Sight   8

The 22nd Century   10

Testimony   13

You Don't Mean That Gesture, She Said   14

On Some Gossip Overheard at the Meritocracy Bar and Grill   15

A True Story That Is Not About Me   17

You Who Are Full of Fear, Fear Not   20

Oh Specious Skies, Our Exit Where?   21

The Magic Puppy Dog Biscuit Predicts the Return of Fall   23

The Shaman Figurine Car Ornament Explains the Accident, Then Naps   24

Rock the Hothouse, Loot the Brain   25

Planetary Notebook   26

Why Are All the Elephants Crying?   28

A Woman Wears a Nose Like a Lost Dwelling   29

At the Evil Boss Convention   31

Portrait on Expired Film   33

Stagflation   34

The Writer's Life   37

And Yes, I Would Like Another Ghost-shaped Truffle!   38

The Lecture 40

Facts for Survival 42

Nostalgia 44

Uniforms Are Sexy Too 46

The Joke 47

By the Skeletons of Hurdygurdy Monkeys and Other Journeys Toward
    Nanotechnology 48

Unnamed Street with Five Fingers and a Box 49

Forgiveness 50

Poem in Favor of Joy 53

Boots, Mistletoe, Cookies and Thumbs 54

Song with Borrowed Shoes 55

This Is What I Meant when I Said My Memories Are Not Exactly True 56

How to Be Happy 57

Fuzzy Parable with Gin Fizz 59

The Joke 60

The Automythologist Takes a Vacation 61

There's No Kindness 62

The Car Door Squeaks Because I'm 32 63

Knots 64

I Don't Live Here Often, She Said 65

A Question 66

For Janet Richmond, Who I Think Hated Elegies 67

Broken Song with Light Bulb Tail 68

Love Song with Loose Toes 70

For Newlyweds 71

"America I have given you all and now I am nothing."

—ALLEN GINSBERG

"And and and. And and and and."

—NOELLE KOCOT

Pageant

The New Realism

It starts when you enter a body of water
named after a forgotten suburb, or when
you tiptoe to the edge of an apartment,
naked, carrying a single egg.

When the New Realism strikes,
you might find yourself listening
to soup evaporate like I did
after every other pleasure failed me

a million times. Try to drape yourself
in Edwardian post-punk glory.
Look into the mirror. Erase the idea
of what you thought of as a self.

Andy Warhol's eyes are now your eyes.
Wear them until they break. Wear
them until they leak. Wear them until
they are your only eyes. Then lose them.

Finally, you will be as profound
as an air conditioner. You will be the negative
space between awkward teeth, the neon fluid
missing from every television sex scene.

Ode to Television

Every morning
is like every night,

except
for you:

a clipped
pause,

a ballerina
passed out

on a chain-
link fence.

Oh beautiful
faux celluloid!

Beautiful
white noise!

Love me
like a fog.

Love me
like the inside

of a bat's
wing—

closed.

The Summer We Were All Seventeen

It was 1968.   The clock read 10:43.

The Vietnam War was trapped in the television

like a moptop Rocky Road ice cream cone.

I was hungry ALL THE TIME,

munching on barbeque-flavored soy chips,

slurping pumpkin ravioli with a trimmed white poodle
named Betty Friedan.

It was the year I found twenty pointy virginities moist
in the fangs of a runaway wolf.

The year my voice broke like a lake and I sang
renegade karaoke naked beneath my sparkly trench coat.

Even the sun was an eyelid—

no one could see the rest of the face.

＊

Dear Radio,
we love you
even though
we all know

you're a big-time phony—
we call you
the secret hiding place
of rock and roll,
but we all know
the real
rock and roll
invented
by Arthur Rimbaud
with flaming tambourines
and multi-breasted albino
oranges
you crushed
years ago,
destroyed with your
beautiful
fangs.

*

In 1968 I was the inventor of bonfires and tie-dyed ball gowns,

the inventor of insomnia and transcendent typos.   Every song ever
played was written by a monkey on a laptop.

Every drum ever destroyed burst with centrifugal liquid lasers.

I was William Carlos Williams dancing
naked in front of the mirror while my wife and children were sleeping.

I was Li Po singing
on the peeling fire escape, smoking pot and cracking jokes about Taoism.

It was 1968 for a whole twenty minutes.

The television broke like fireworks.   The television
exploded
                                                                    like sprinklers.

It was 1968 for a whole century.   It was 1968
when we made love beneath
                                        the rainbow canopy of candy GI Joes

and gave birth to a Janis Joplin Cabbage Patch Doll.

Jimi Hendrix swallowed
the ashes and dove headfirst into the My Little Pony blow-up pool.

I was twenty years old
or I was six years old.   I devoured every radio,
                                                    eating the wires.

I hooked my veins to the electrical current
                              and wrote emails to Gilgamesh twenty-four hours a day.

I illegally downloaded *Steal This Book*.

I fell down on the green carpet and stared at my bedroom's cloud wallpaper.

I saw my face forming in every two-dimensional puff.

It was the summer
of free vowels,

damp noses,   exfoliating

participles.

I was nostalgic for the idea of poetry

more than poetry itself.

I injected caesuras into the veins of my toy cadaver

and wrote the word "revolution"   all over my friend's plaster cast.

Rain-soaked toddlers photographed me

and sold the negatives on Ebay.

I covered every centimeter of my body   with discarded gum wrappers.

I covered my head with a floating chuppa and sewed a colorful bikini

out of a discarded hijab.

I wore the whole city around my waist as a dangling belt.

Everyone could hear me   jangling

from the other side of the globe.

Plain Sight

I hid the 20th century
in my Marcel Duchamp lunchbox.
I hid the First War in a crate labeled
Second War. I hid my tears
in a fuzzy rat slipper
with bulging eyes and a Pepto-Bismol mouth.
I hid my screaming in a poem
about a popping toaster.
I hid Eva Braun's marzipan earlobes
in calla lily bouquets, dripping
with cubic zirconium solitaires.
I hid love, hate, happiness and fear
in the words *love, hate, happiness*
and *fear.* I hid my extra nipple
in the elevator on the thirteenth floor.
(Marked 14.) I hid my Jewishness
in a bowl of *treyf* matzo ball soup.
I hid my tongue in a dear reader's mouth.
I hid the memory of Rrose Sélavy
(ripped wig and melting lipstick)
in a reality show about thousand-dollar
commodes. I hid the bleeding
turkey in a package of Tofurky.
I hid my fat in polka-dot pantyhose.
I hid my love for you in a story
about a haunted swing. (I erased
the suicidal dove epilogue.) I hid
my fake mustache in a G-string
in Texas. I hid my revolutionary

pedagogy in a paper on Marxist clowns.
I hid my mucus in transformational Formica.
I hid my blood in a vial of cranberry cocktail.
I hid my small breasts in a bra padded
with Cracker Jacks. I hid the soldier's
finger in a marble cake chess piece,
the cigarette posed on the dead Iraqi's mouth
in a case plated with fake gold.
(That was our "first" Gulf War.)
I hid the headless legless female torso
in the body of a real live girl! I hid
the runaway sperm in a plastic cowboy hat,
the surrealist revolver in a paisley beanbag.
I hid all the missing bodies in the belly
of a sleeping tuba. I hid everything in crushed
Diet Coke cans, in Ouija boards made out
of M&M boxes, in language transparent as clear
plastic chairs, in french fries and fried idealism,
in rain falling on sinking Southwestern shopping centers,
in empty Doritos bags full of alien orange powder.

The 22nd Century

We wander, decorating fingernails
with designer bacteria, adorning
earlobes with the borrowed limbs
of embalmed neurosurgeons.

No one is sad.
No one knows the word sad.
The 21st century sleeps
hidden in its permeable shell.

Every mystery novel ends
with an opaque coffee stain.
Every love story—
a missing tongue.

Testimony

I wasn't trying to satirize early 21st century
masculinity when I twisted your Velcro nipple
and ripped open the time/space continuum
so that my favorite robot cuckoo could escape
being cajoled by every two-bit canary.
Okay, so it wasn't sincerity either. Not exactly.
If by sincerity you mean the early morning dew
rising from the untouched piano keys, that moment
when you realize you are not only capable of closing
your eyes at that boring movie, but also alone
in your one-room apartment with your broken
telescopes and unwashed ice cream dishes.

You see, I was only trying to understand
what America must feel like after all the boys
and girls have left the classroom, and all
the street lights are turned off to allow
for the multiplying of what will come to be
labeled "private space." I just wanted to know
how the doctors felt after they finished sterilizing
the chess pieces and how the teachers felt after
they wrapped the last of the janitors' nosebleeds.
More than anything, I wanted to understand how
it might feel to be inside and outside at the exact
same moment. Would it be like holding a ladybug
in one's open palm, or would it be more like
the feeling of singing as you watch the last
audience member turn his back to the stage?

You Don't Mean That Gesture, She Said

The house made of bird-of-paradise fronds
kicked me out. Its walls said, Go teach
Frederick Douglass to the mice in the tundra
and sing of shackles in ice-castle mansions.
Bring kneepads to pray to the hydrogen icon
and lower your head like a mediocre lover,
bee keeper, vaudeville star. Ha ha ha ha he he
he he, said the bellicose walls as they spun toward
the walls of the dictator's house, the house inside
a hot pink artery, the house made of burning
whatevers, fuck you little girly, little girl, said
the windows of the house that wouldn't let me in,
said the prisoners of the house, the house made
of pepper, made of pepper, diamonds and tin cans.

On Some Gossip Overheard at the Meritocracy Bar and Grill

I've heard the rich do not exist,
that they vanished with the chimeras
and the Peanut Butter Oompas
when the asteroid hit their numinous
skeletal sky yacht, so now the rich
are no more real than the non-rich,
who wait for the F train to take them
to their jobs as pedicab drivers or
Adjunct Assistant Blindfolded Archery
Professors at nomadic colleges.
Still, even if the rich do not exist,
they still exist in everyone's heart,
like a precocious fifth grader's idea of God,
malleable to any idealistic or corrupt
imagination, a different connotation
in every language: an untranslatable
poem set to a thousand different tunes,
each urging us to join by singing,
"The rich are a new brand of sneakers.
The rich are my favorite rock band.
The rich know how to throw a war."
Those rich, always polishing
their oil tanker Christmas ornaments,
always blowing on each other's
nose jobs, always transforming
into scurrying nanobots, roving
inside the organs of the rarest elephants,
the test tubes of the future genius,

the Nasdaq's bloodless veins—
and then out, plopped out
again, so they are still the rich,
dropped into the muddy puddle
they like to call "The Soul,"
copyright 2006, patent pending.

A True Story That Is Not About Me

    1) alarm clocks fall out windows …

They fall into stock pots   into soup,
boiling soup

        into black square
        puddles

        with sharp edges,
        exposed brains

        hooked to wires—

The black square shifts
when we talk about it.

(Talk about them?)

The pots empty   invisible

all hail the black square   squares
the black square   hail hail.

We listen to the swish
of glass squares switching hands.

All hail the black squares.

Hailed and hailed.

2) this used to be a poem about robot pigeons

But now, it's a poem about money like all poems
written in Microsoft Word in early twenty-first
century late-capitalist Brooklyn. It's Yom Kippur

and I cancelled class and said I'd be at services,
but I'm at home in our bedroom/office/laundry-paper-
chaos generator trying not to think about eating,

even though I've never in my whole life fasted.
No one in my family fasts. Outside, Con Edison
is drilling again, windows shake from the blast.

3) did you hear that?

The truth is
I am always happier
as someone else.

My body floated in ether.
Other bodies
knocked about

bloated and orange
like Tang floating
through a feeding tube.

I was happy then,
slightly neon, slightly
Pavlovian and damp.

You Who Are Full of Fear, Fear Not

The world kept urging me
to wear more orange—

do a little flaming hula dance,
cha cha cha and so on.

*

It's kind of like
what they say
about the kind
leading the kind.

*

There's a tack in every moving plan.

A culture of what?

A culture of the.

It.

Oh Specious Skies, Our Exit Where?

The pageant is performed
by cats and babies dressed
as soldiers. We are the only audience.

You are Charlie Brown
and I am Charlie Brown.

There is only a mirror keeping us
apart, making this a star-crossed
love story of sorts.

In matching zigzag sweaters
with lipless mouths,
we hum anthems,

chomp on popcorn and
deactivated sparkless Pop Rocks.
Our blank eyes gape.

A young boy in a patchwork flag
descends on a rocking horse
suspended from the domed ceiling.

His voice booms, "You may be
Charlie Brown, but that doesn't mean
I am also Charlie Brown."

There are guns bopping in glitter tutus.
There are tanks cobbled together
from deconstructed Barbie Dream Houses.

The projected subtitles say
We are not the audience.
We are not even Charlie Brown.

We are Lucy!

Lucy of cream pies
and poems hidden
in Hello Kitty mittens.

Lucy, dressed in her dented
halo made of wild car antennas.

The pageant text is a scrambled
signal poorly deciphered by an infant
in a lilac evening gown.

The pageant's music is an echo of fingers
typing the numbers in a backward
Fibonacci sequence.

You are Lucy and I am Lucy,
and thank God we are Lucy,

and not that boy on the rocking horse
floating above us, mumbling

a lullaby as he pulls hair
out of his battered doll.

The Magic Puppy Dog Biscuit Predicts the Return of Fall

After a week in silence and catatonic gloaming,
a parakeet chirps, a clown room-divider opens
his eyes letting light in and dragonflies out.

This is the sort of day needed to grow justice,
I write on my lover's tongue, convinced
that the feel of it will be enough to make it true.

The Shaman Figurine Car Ornament Explains the Accident, Then Naps

We were lured by color:
the only periwinkle left
in the decomposing empire—
I mean, restaurant,
     so we opened it—
allowed a light to circumnavigate
the dancer's limb, allowed
     a margin to expand,
     past the fleshy cylinder,
     back to the migrating parts.

Rock the Hothouse, Loot the Brain

The woman who denies the inevitability of television
is using a bluejay for a cell phone.

Figures.

Does this make her a prodigal rock star?

Is she the wayward audience God sent
to bash my guitar?

Oh,
       just say yeah,

say "day" and mean
let's end the frickin' yap-yap.
Finally get some sushi!

It's like when I was waiting
for the vacuum cleaner salesman
to rush into the room and save me
from music, or the years I wasted
as a teenage bounty hunter.

Life is just a bumper sticker,
I write on a bumper sticker—

you and me and the other me
fight for the pillow.

Planetary Notebook

"Even my dead mother has a body double,"
    or "even my body double is a version of my dead mother."

Are these the words of the hit manifesto
conquering the exurbs
    or just another crazy lady

lecturing the morning subway riders
on the minutiae
    of metaphysical gossip?

Either way,
the moon is just
a radish stem, or the moon
is just
    a semantic marker.
    Here,
we say
    or *here.*

   *

"Do you still think anything is possible?"

"No, I do not think anything is possible."

"Do you think it is possible to hold your elbow to the third rail
and feel an oncoming disaster?"

"No, I think each sadness is unique like each February."

"Do you think a photocopy of a snowflake is more beautiful than the original?"

"No, I think that opera is only one of many strategies to combat happiness."

"Could you pretend you feel more than the newspaper allows?"

"No, but if I ever awake to my own sobbing, the cherry tree might sing like an anvil."

Why Are All the Elephants Crying?

I am wrinkle-free,
which isn't a problem
except for the clock bird
trapped in my curls.
It's been on fire
for a while now,
which makes
my stepparents
ramp up
our insurance policies
and enroll me
in a clone school
where no one looks
the same
though
everyone is.

A Woman Wears a Nose Like a Lost Dwelling

she says *here is my nose*
my second home
here is the bird
that pecks at it
here is the camera
that scares
the bird that pecks
at my nose
at the house
on my face...

I am the woman's boss
I ride in a helicopter
with all
the windows open
as if I am the only god
that matters
I wear a towel
around my neck
a blanket
over my knees
and I laugh
at her nose
at her house
of a nose
and the bird
that pecks
at her
nose-house

and at
the picture
of her
now ripped
lost in
tangible air

At the Evil Boss Convention

They are plucking live chickens again—
or so the official website claims.

In reality, they are stretching out.
Their shoes already off,

they watch the spider webs
expanding between their

spread toes, admire the intricate
work of the most practical of arts.

Being an evil boss used to be easier.
There used to be places to go:

evil boss clam shacks
and evil boss barbershops

full of evil boss funhouse mirrors
and evil boss double-jointed scissors.

To be an evil boss in the century of evil
bosses was to meander the avenue.

Oh how they would yodel back then—
showing off the full range of their robot falsettos,

decked out in their finest evil boss
metallic rubber togas, their gold-plated

bat-shaped fang-augmented slippers,
their super-genius evil boss grins.

Portrait on Expired Film

She wears her hair in a halo of dollar bills,
calls herself by her enemy's name

Struck a bargain for sure.

Lost as a helium cloud or a dozen
lips bulging in all the wrong places.

Roar.
Whatever.

How often can she fling herself
at the divine without chipping a nail?

She's like the girl who sings the words
money is abstract at the multiplex

before a car crash and a synthesized tune
destroys the truth of a denuded screen.

Stagflation

When the rent went up, we shifted
all motion west, lifted the bottoms
of our pant legs as if crossing a creek.

No one cared that our poems were made
of torqued magnetic force or that our
hands could translate the language of light

into a million fractured dialects. We still
had to climb. Like every other army of bald
Rapunzels scaling the leaning tower of Babel.

When the rent doubled, we drew smiles
around our real smiles, curtsied our way
into the arms of identical semiotics experts

who changed our names to fit the texture
of the times, tucked in our billowing tunics,
whipped our hair into vertical configurations,

—blond Aqua-Netted beehives—tall enough
to pass through the school's cracked skylight,
to reach the blimps inching through the noise.

The Writer's Life

To be a writer is to apply lotion to one's forehead

to sing untranslatable lullabies to brussels sprouts.

Writing in sunlight is a good way to get a tan.

Be kind to the commas,

like you they would rather be curled up in a fetal position.

If you plan to write about sex,
make sure you've had it,

at least once.

If you plan to write about politics,
make sure your poem

is softer than an eyelid,
louder than a nuclear volcano.

And Yes, I Would Like Another
Ghost-shaped Truffle!

The pink plastic skulls at the proofreader's
Halloween party are lit with flickering candles,
and I think I would be happy to do nothing
but stare at them, transported into a liminal
state of wavering light, but then there's that voice,
that high-pitched shriek of that woman across
the table, her face thick with orange-tinted beige,
her hair helmeted with mousse, that voice:
a Long Island screeching highway, even though
she says she's lived in New Rochelle for many years.
As I down red wine, the windows wavering,
she keeps blabbing about her work as a shaman-
in-training, her glorious apprenticeship
in past life regression. Everyone is talking
about their journeys: their trips in zero gravity
immersion tanks, their swallowing of microscopic
biological crystals, their lifelong study into
the subtleties of aromatherapy. Just so you know,
if you take a certain cocktail of psychotropic drugs
in a locked gymnasium in the suburban woods,
the men who catch your projectile vomit in buckets
are called Angels. As I listen to the overlapping stories,
a woman keeps double-dipping her carrot in the packaged
hummus. The man who wanted to be an artist is talking
about his life as a sports photographer, what lenses
are needed to capture sweat. Everyone is trying so hard
to be happy—I am eating too much spider web-motif
chocolate cake and ersatz Reese's peanut butter balls

wrapped to look like bloody eyes. Everyone else is stuffing
their mouths with potato chips, talking about how they don't
want to overindulge as they overindulge, patting their flat
or bulging bellies as they expand in the black spandexed night.
A woman across the room dressed like a sexed-up pirate
is talking about genital piercing, the stuffed parrot on her
shoulder shaking at her every word, and I am feeling a little
repulsed at the thought of her clitoris or any clitoris exposed
under the red light of the highway piercing parlor, all the strangers
in the dim waiting room turning the pages of celebrity magazines
hearing her yell out, and yeah, I know my revulsion is not
a very compassionate emotion—and I remember once seeing
the number of Americans who are into genital piercing
and thinking that there are more people who are into genital piercing
than read contemporary poetry or read *any* poetry—
just like there are more marketing specialists who get off on
dressing up as Anime characters for toy robot conventions
at highway Hiltons or join clubs to develop their skills in pet ESP
or drink neon-blue Mentos-flavored martinis while they trade stories
about the years they spent selling dancing-Snoopy-decorated bongs,
imitation Guatemalan glow-in-the-dark worry dolls and waterproof
guides to automotive meditation from the back of their "My Son Is
an Honor Student" and "I Vote for Jesus" bumper-stickered vans.

The Lecture

"We are waiting for a dog with a tennis ball
or some other break in the grand Western expanse,"

I explain to the crowd of fidgeting students
on the twentieth floor of the once-full school.

"Listen for the squeak," I urge them.
Listen to the rain plopping on silk apple

blossoms like in that poster of your
favorite painting not yet completely

ruined by its location in the steamy dentist office.
Yes, I know the color of my necktie looks

better wearing 3-D goggles. I've known
for years that Ms. Winnie Alvarez has

declared me the teacher least likely to get laid
and that the cord spiraling out of my brain socket

is not some cute ornament designed by elfin
cosmopolites, but is in fact a truth-antenna

hooked into every fluctuation in the school's
atmosphere, even the curve of your mouth

forming the curse of my name, even the soft silk
rustle between the gym teacher's opaline thighs.

That is why my smile always looks applied by
a makeup artist who snorts too much Picasso

and why when I laugh it's not a full-bodied let-the-ocean-
destroy-the-bamboo-shack-that-was-my-soul brand roar,

but a docile micro-gurgle,
almost a gulp.

Facts for Survival

I read somewhere that Juicy Fruit,
that flat enigma of condensed nostalgia,
tastes best in winter on the beach
when the ship's deck is cleaned by animatronic flies.
This is why no one believes in love anymore.
We can still feel it in our toes, the emotion
lifting the ceiling towards the giant swans,
but the *idea* of love has vanished like a smell.
We carry within us our "lowly origins,"
or is it our "lively organs?" Something or other
is wriggling through our rib cages.
There's nothing glamorous about muck,
even if it's well lit as in Film Noir.
But, yes, I have seen people sitting on curbs,
planning temporary revolutions to coincide
with Macy's yearly white sale. I've seen
their jewel-like flames cracking apart and tried
to steal the shards to get us high.
Beauty and terror—terror and beauty—
those would be good names if I ever
adopted a pair of puppy schnauzers.
Truth is, I *have* in some private moments
felt the power of the Shekinah lurking in
an empty Aunt Jemima-shaped bottle,
but being hungry always makes me
too distracted to write anything profound.
I'd rather just damn the pancakes
and stuff my face with soy bacon.

The noble purpose needed to achieve
completion is, as you imagined, kaput.
I'm sorry, I borrowed it when I ran out
of baking power and wanted the muffins
to rise. I'm also sorry to hear you've
become a grotesque mirror of your mom.
But it's really not so bad. *Is it?*
At least your mother knew how
to clean a coffee pot, which is more
than I could say for your dad.

for Sharon Mesmer

Nostalgia

I was the best ukulele smasher
at the Cedar Hills Outlet Mall.
A dynamo of musical strangulation,
I dazzled all those strangers

at the Cedar Hills Outlet Mall,
frozen like a pizza circa 1986.
I dazzled all those strangers,
little girls with Halloween teeth.

Frozen like a pizza circa 1986,
springy-antennae UFO headbands,
little girls with Halloween teeth
always swinging their Nerf swords.

Springy-antennae UFO headbands
bobbing above pigtailed sweeties
always swinging their Nerf swords,
gussied up in neon tube socks.

Bobbing above pigtailed sweeties
like love itself freed from language.
Gussied up in neon tube socks,
kids dashed up the broken escalator.

Like love itself freed from language,
a politics removed from the music of event.
Kids dashed up the broken escalator,
swaying to the Christmas sing-a-long.

A politics removed from the music of event,
a song that ends on the note it began.
Swaying to the Christmas sing-a-long
I tried to bop to the anemic beats.

A song that ends on the note it began,
a dynamo of musical strangulation.
I tried to bop to the anemic beats.
I was the best ukulele smasher.

Uniforms Are Sexy Too

A bottle of old cough syrup
gels on a windowsill.
I walk on tiptoes
as if wearing
invisible stilettos.

You think any old bottle opener
can open a dream.

So there.
So what.

The color red means more to me
than the smell
of a beautiful
crash.

The Joke

The last joke in the world finds itself in the womb of a pregnant Jamie Lynn Spears.

"Knock. Knock." It bangs against the uterus walls.

No one answers. The video feed from the Second World War is projected on the outside of a wiggling fallopian tube.

Bodies. Wire. Burning. Ash.

Terrible silence rules.

Before it was a fetus, the joke had wanted to be a poem.

It used to watch the lyrics line up between the toy boats in the still lake.

It envied their decorum, the way their sails billowed when the children blew.

By the Skeletons of Hurdygurdy Monkeys and Other Journeys Toward Nanotechnology

We were trying to truth-squad
the peanut,
feng-shui the inside of a mitten
when a translucent
figure descended,
slipped between our necks
and breath cavities
making our lips too heavy
to rest on the rim
of any teacup. So then,
the black rapids roared,
overflowing
every daydream
and backyard pool.

Unnamed Street with Five Fingers and a Box

I watch the drunk shirtless gods
clean windows. A girl in white gloves
sniffs a gold-plated soapbox.

I'm all eyelids again. My cell phone
pretends it's a sick bird, sobbing
elevator music in my crowded pocket.

Hey, have you ever seen a decapitated
butterfly? They say it looks like any other.
On television, the crowd chants

and for once, I embrace the moment,
accept the burgeoning and bulging
multitude, their beautiful demands.

Forgiveness

In every poem titled "Forgiveness,"
it is snowing. Even if the poem
is set in Florida, and the theorist
on the beach is brushing sand
off his sun-kissed Speedo.
Even if the poem is written
at a table lit by candlelight
with a feather pen dipped
in red wine, fathoms beneath
a smoldering volcano.

If the poem is called
"Forgiveness" snow must fall
on the neck of a porcelain figurine,
must cover the closed eyes
of a woman silently thinking
of screaming and how wonderful
it would feel to stroke each
imaginary yell.
Roll it out. *Become as elastic as*
a dismembered paper clip,
I would tell her.

Poem in Favor of Joy

I was happy
to be empty
a nude economy

oh, for you,
you alone,
I ended

my lifetime
ban on
men

let's just
say the DNA
island ends

here

Boots, Mistletoe, Cookies and Thumbs

Yesterday we almost rose, snakelike evergreens
in the haze, plastic chains around the hippo
we assumed was evening, and cuddled with our
quiet songs. Yesterday, we were almost sad:
all the elderberries tasted like rotting tomatilloes,
all the bite-sized babies rolled in powdered sugar
for the lullaby hour. I was almost naked then,
plagued by bloody water fountains and serenading
gargoyles, by a flaming red foot from the Yucatan
and another from a stable in the northwest Bronx.
Did I want it to end? Did I really want it to end?
I just wanted a you, *to be* a you—a pair of eyes,
unleashed by books and brackish lightning,
merry-go-rounds, whirling in unbound snow.

Song with Borrowed Shoes

Like any other woman,
I'm tricky—
a songless cricket.

I name my needle
Patience and wait
for the wet thistle

to turn into crowbar
penitence, into cellophane
or liquid glass, into

cracked ceramic dice,
a pair of muffled
cymbals, a knife.

This Is What I Meant when I Said My Memories Are Not Exactly True

plow off every helmet until your metal tongue
blasts open your head
        ride your humpback
all over the green metallic dunes
behind an eye forest ? stumps
wet hives   *albino pigeons*
no, nothing is ever said or sad
no, I never wear blue jeans to sleep

the window opens on a back alley
dueling bagpipers practice a duende
version of "Sweet Home Alabama"

        floating macaroni Brooklyn street life
is all I can think   no clue why or if
a puffy-head muffin might as well
own every so-called "emotion"

what is a puffy-head muffin anyway?

it's like love she said,
packaged to sell

How to Be Happy

Imagine yourself as a grandfather clock:

the last left standing in the eye
of the micro-Apocalypse.

When everyone is sleeping
you flap—

a wet gum wrapper
or a phantom woolly mammoth.

It would be as if every fruit bat
understood the limit of light,

felt the secret of career explosion,
squirreled away in salt and pepper shakers.

When I was a gnat, this was easier to explain.

When I was an ogre, no one asked me to file

my taxes or rearrange my logical
positivism into a good or bad column.

Love, like any other time of day,
expanded and doubled over.

We poured science-fiction-themed
operas out of every pore and squeezed

our eyes until sweet wine flowed
out of every broken faucet.

Fuzzy Parable with Gin Fizz

I spot my ex-boyfriend's girlfriend's cat, June,
crawling my pink skyscraper. Imagine the stress.
Her cat. *My* once-growing empire. The damn moon
advertising the beast's mistake. Oh how I obsess!
"My skyscraper!" *"Her* cat!" *"My* snake-
like tower!" A once-grand idea of ownership now moot
as the couple on a perfectly decorated wedding cake
devoured by drunk guests. "It was a beaut,"
I mumble to the cha-cha-ing dumbwaiter, puzzled as Garbo
watching the T-shirt versions of her visage play
Marco Polo on the bulbous chests of every hobo.
What a century! What a cat! What a day!
I can't help it. That spire's mucous rhinestones
are my gems! Mere roses stink compared to their cologne.

The Joke

A standup comedian tells a joke in the basement of an abandoned theater. None of the windows laugh. A red curtain yells out, *I know you always hated your mother.* A broken mug on the unplugged television set pretends to cry by chipping its sides. This is the start of poetry and the end of sleep. The ex-comedian shows up years later, a fat man in a pink dress, top button replaced by a gaping black hole. He's slept too long under decaying bridges. His eyes have been replaced with apparition-rendering devices. His nose is the birthplace of an alternate earth. His audience is way past bored. They don't want to hear about his time as a fern psychotherapist or his method of detaching souls from picked-over lettuce carcasses. They don't want to learn about the proper way to float in radioactive ectoplasm. All they want is to seep into his skin, rename his organs after their childhood pals. They just long to see his cells splitting open, to hear their own voices, rattling in his cavernous mouth.

The Automythologist Takes a Vacation

All love stories begin with a coat rack,
a coat rack sutured with wire,
or a coat rack, a coat rack hanging
above an alabaster chicken field.

It's not just love,
these coat racks.

All friendships begin with a coat rack, too.
Baby coat racks, smelling of talcum,
talismanic coat racks dripping with coins.

＊

Mechanical birds. Tree tribes. Speech.

Yup. Sad.

That's almost   about it.
Like me

going all postal
on the snow brigade.

＊

Much ado about handstands.
Much ado about the wonderful
smell of a lead pencil.

Consider the possibility of crossing.
Consider that the soul was once
just another red sled.
Red, pumped—

the only toothache
among the pared-down stars.

There's No Kindness

in water vapor doing
what I am afraid to be

sure, I could write
a love poem and appear

triumphantly daft
or a business letter,

perfectly adroit, confident,
a wingless fly scurrying

over an air conditioner
makes the afternoon

less than praiseworthy
to the fanatically clean,

but not to me,
a veritable believer

in the inherent
glamour of error

The Car Door Squeaks Because I'm 32

I am in love, so I should be happy.
I am losing money, so I should be sad,
my Being the supposed center
of all cause, oceanic in a kitchen-
sink-Brooklyn-tenement-
apartment sense—my skin
reborn as bourgeois gesture,
the line connecting my flesh
to my flesh as well as to
the toothbrush aisle
in the drugstore. Look—
a series of Russian dolls:
a sad doll inside a happy doll
inside a sad doll inside a happy
child inside a racecar inside
an empty elephant inside
the idea of happiness,
a one-winged sparrow,
morning glory ape brains,
fabulous jelly donuts and
sunrise for breakfast poured...

Knots

Spacious and knobby as the mounds
of rust-colored Albuquerque
or the last crinkly leaves
suspended from December trees,
I'm so neutral it almost hurts.
As I walk, dusk creeps,
imperceptible specks take off,
as if they were spit-out watermelon seeds
or an eclipsed arch spiraling
at the edge of the seen
like me, unaligned, barely
half-massed, passing a damp,
discarded *New York Post* flattened
in the street, the edge
of a woman's symmetrical face,
and the headline: SLAIN DANCER,
her topless secret now covered
with muddy footprints,
a straw wrapper,
two finger-shaped twigs.

I Don't Live Here Often, She Said

Found tonsils.

Caterpillar skin.

A left-tit-right-tit binary code.

More excuses for a conversation
not to have.

A canal through a sewer.

You know how it is.

A Question

"Is one still kosher
if they replace
part of your heart
with a pig's?"
my mother jokes
about her upcoming
aortic surgery.
As I listen
to her laugh,
I feel my own heart
coming apart;
it hurts,
tottering
in my chest
like a working class
fashionista,
fake leather
stilettos
wobbling up
the subway's
broken
wet
escalator.

For Janet Richmond, Who I Think Hated Elegies

Tiny kumquat slumber squalor the sun was
is always pounding out the rhythm of your heart
(or is it art). You were more alive than tofu
wiggling on the music stand or your poems
breaking frou-frou wings as they pushed punk
sparkling blades through the crowded aisle
to the red yellow periwinkle purple blue red
green puce everything anything inside the universal
thumbprint (yours?) The great he said she said
la la la la of it and you writing painting laughing
praising from your ashes live action notes on the waste
can's epidermis live action words on the surface
of the earth's rough tongue live action chopsticks
rubbed together on the bottom of your flaming boots.

Broken Song with Light Bulb Tail

I was the sleeper,
dreaming of sleep.

My husband slept
in a soft shoe, but only

when the moon was red
or the shoe blue.

There was never any closure
at the end of sleep, just more sleep.

Everything was left
undone.

That wasn't a blue jay
trapped in the picture of a tree.

It was the word
"blue jay"

drifting around
the runaway eye.

The dragon was sleeping
in the word,

curled up
like a kitten.

Some nights
we drifted in a raft,

over the ocean
made of eyes.

I loved all verbs equally,
as a good mother should.

In the house, I asked
the walls to testify.

One said "yellow."
Another "yes."

for David Shapiro

Love Song with Loose Toes

Whenever you
are midnight blue
pigeon-footed-
morning, I am the notes
of the unplugged
guitar, singing like
a spoon in a hot
pot, singing like
a heap of wet laundry.

"Is this how to be
when bees leave?"

a note written inside
a word written about
somebody else's inside.

It started in the dark.
It started dark—

swallows' claws,
your hands,

a snowy hovel.

for Bob

For Newlyweds

Walk to each other, slowly,
as if in a field of flowering microchips.

Your refection will soon be clarified
in the mirror of a gleaming cleaver.

Watch it magnified, stretched out
by the processed moonlight.

You will never again remember
how it feels to be alone, what you

thought about as you listened to
the crackling of the radio asteroids.

Your lips will never again dry up.
Your nose will never again be mistaken

for a curved ashtray or a slender
eggplant, falling off a shelf.

Love, you will call your new self,
as if it were a stuffed penguin.

Love, you will call the windowpane
cracked from all the years you tried

to use it as a door. So long little cup,
twisted like a face. So long little bird,

smashed inside an ear. If you dream
of yourself holding hands with a ghost,

twist off its head and pour out the steaming
liquid within. If you dream of a city

crawling with enormous muddy tubes,
be aware that robot rulers are always blind.

They can't see you sticking out your tongue
or making a model of the local anchorwoman

so you can hide her behind the wet
shower curtain when the bombs fall.

Despite what the song lyrics say,
this is how marriage was meant to be:

a man and a woman, or a woman and a woman,
or a chair and a table, or a tulip and a shattered vase.

It's all the same. Write your vows as if they were
written in invisible ink. Write your vows as if

they were made out of cloud intestines and loose
change, as if they were made to be sung by a choir

of swaddled infants. Bid goodbye to the bumpy
pillow stuffed with pay stubs and counterfeit bills.

Goodbye to the dusty kitty you'd pet on your way
to the twenty-four hour butcher-slash-discothèque.

Your new life starts by unraveling the light.
Your new life starts you when you bash your

shadow with a kite. It really starts *here*:
on this airplane with all the empty seats,

flying over a city that used to have another name,
used to be full of taller and/or skinnier buildings,

used to be teeming with houseplants, bursting
with rollerblading messengers, brimming with lakes.

NOTES

*

"For Janet Richmond, Who I Think Hated Elegies" is for Janet Richmond, a poet who died in December 1804.

"Facts for Survival" and "Broken Song with Light Bulb Tail" were written by answering questions in poems by Sharon Mesmer ("What Becomes Us") and David Shapiro ("Questions for You").

RECENT TITLES FROM
ALICE JAMES BOOKS

The Bitter Withy, Donald Revell
Winter Tenor, Kevin Goodan
Slamming Open the Door, Kathleen Sheeder Bonanno
Rough Cradle, Betsy Sholl
Shelter, Carey Salerno
The Next Country, Idra Novey
Begin Anywhere, Frank Giampietro
The Usable Field, Jane Mead
King Baby, Lia Purpura
The Temple Gate Called Beautiful, David Kirby
Door to a Noisy Room, Peter Waldor
Beloved Idea, Ann Killough
The World in Place of Itself, Bill Rasmovicz
Equivocal, Julie Carr
A Thief of Strings, Donald Revell
Take What You Want, Henrietta Goodman
The Glass Age, Cole Swensen
The Case Against Happiness, Jean-Paul Pecqueur
Ruin, Cynthia Cruz
Forth A Raven, Christina Davis
The Pitch, Tom Thompson
Landscapes I & II, Lesle Lewis
Here, Bullet, Brian Turner
The Far Mosque, Kazim Ali
Gloryland, Anne Marie Macari
Polar, Dobby Gibson
Pennyweight Windows: New & Selected Poems, Donald Revell
Matadora, Sarah Gambito
In the Ghost-House Acquainted, Kevin Goodan
The Devotion Field, Claudia Keelan
Into Perfect Spheres Such Holes Are Pierced, Catherine Barnett
Goest, Cole Swensen

Alice James Books has been publishing exclusively poetry since 1973. One of the few presses in the country that is run collectively, the cooperative selects manuscripts for publication through both regional and national annual competitions. New regional authors become active members of the cooperative, participating in the editorial decisions of the press. The press, which historically has placed an emphasis on publishing women poets, was named for Alice James, sister of William and Henry, whose fine journal and gift for writing went unrecognized within her lifetime.

TYPESET AND DESIGNED BY MARY AUSTIN SPEAKER

PRINTED BY THOMSON-SHORE
ON 30% POSTCONSUMER RECYCLED PAPER
PROCESSED CHLORINE-FREE